God is within Her

COLOURING THE PSALMS FOR WOMEN

This Colouring Book
Belongs To:

Welcome

Welcome to your God is Within Her Colouring the Psalms for women, colouring book. This colouring book is designed to help you pray the psalms while relaxing by colouring key phrases.

It has 30 Psalms for your to colour, as well as excerpts from the Psalm that you can read, pray and contemplate.

As you colour, allow the words to bring you God's Peace and His Joy!

Happy Colouring!

God is our refuge and strength,
an ever-present help in trouble.
Therefore we will not fear,
though the earth give way
and the mountains fall into the heart of the sea,
though its waters roar and foam
and the mountains quake with their surging.
There is a river whose streams
make glad the city of God,
the holy place where the Most High dwells.
God is within her, she will not fall;
God will help her at break of day.
Nations are in uproar, kingdoms fall;
he lifts his voice, the earth melts.
The Lord Almighty is with us;
the God of Jacob is our fortress.
Come and see what the Lord has done,
the desolations he has brought on the earth.
He makes wars cease
to the ends of the earth.
He breaks the bow and shatters the spear;
he burns the shields with fire.
He says, "Be still, and know that I am God;
I will be exalted among the nations, I will be exalted in the earth."
The Lord Almighty is with us;
the God of Jacob is our fortress.

PSALM 46

God is within Her, she will not fall.
PSALM 46:5

Blessed be the Lord,

for he has wondrously shown

his steadfast love to me

when I was beset as a city under siege.

I had said in my alarm,

"I am driven far from your sight."

But you heard my supplications

when I cried out to you for help.

Love the Lord, all you his saints.

The Lord preserves the faithful,

but abundantly repays

the one who acts haughtily.

Be strong, and let your heart

take courage,

all you who wait for the Lord.

PSALM 31:21-24

I will sing praise
to the name
of the Lord,
the Most High.
Psalm 7:17

Trust in the Lord, and do good;

so you will live in the land,

and enjoy security.

Take delight in the Lord,

and he will give you

the desires of your heart.

Commit your way to the Lord;

trust in him, and he will act.

He will make your vindication

shine like the light,

and the justice of your cause

like the noonday.

Be still before the Lord,

and wait patiently for him;

do not fret over those

who prosper in their way,

over those who carry out evil devices.

PSALM 26:10

DELIGHT IN THE
Lord,
& HE WILL GIVE YOU THE
desires
OF YOUR
heart.
PSALM 37:4

I will give thanks to the Lord with my whole heart;

I will tell of all your wonderful deeds.

I will be glad and exult in you;

I will sing praise to your name, O Most High.

When my enemies turned back,

they stumbled and perished before you.

For you have maintained my just cause;

you have sat on the throne giving righteous judgment.

You have rebuked the nations,

you have destroyed the wicked;

you have blotted out their name forever and ever.

The enemies have vanished in everlasting ruins;

their cities you have rooted out;

the very memory of them has perished.

But the Lord sits enthroned forever,

he has established his throne for judgment.

He judges the world with righteousness;

he judges the peoples with equity.

PSALM 9:1-8

I WILL
give thanks
TO THE LORD
WITH MY WHOLE HEART;
I WILL TELL OF ALL THY
wonderful
deeds
PSALM 9:1

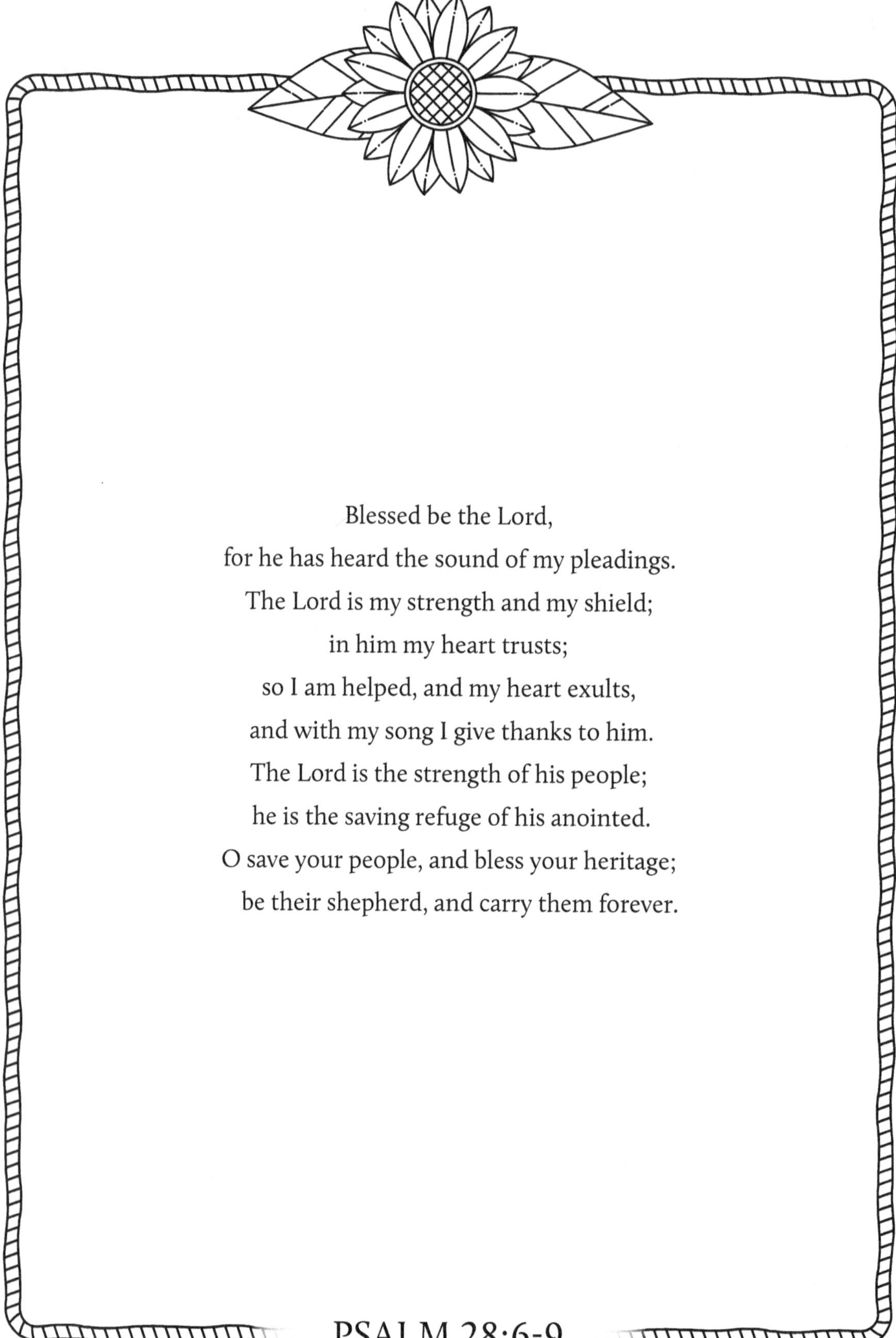

Blessed be the Lord,

for he has heard the sound of my pleadings.

The Lord is my strength and my shield;

in him my heart trusts;

so I am helped, and my heart exults,

and with my song I give thanks to him.

The Lord is the strength of his people;

he is the saving refuge of his anointed.

O save your people, and bless your heritage;

be their shepherd, and carry them forever.

PSALM 28:6-9

THE LORD IS MY
strength &
MY *shield*;
IN HIM MY HEART
trusts;
SO I AM HELPED,
& MY HEART
exults,
AND WITH MY SONG
I GIVE *thanks*
TO HIM.
PSALM 28:7

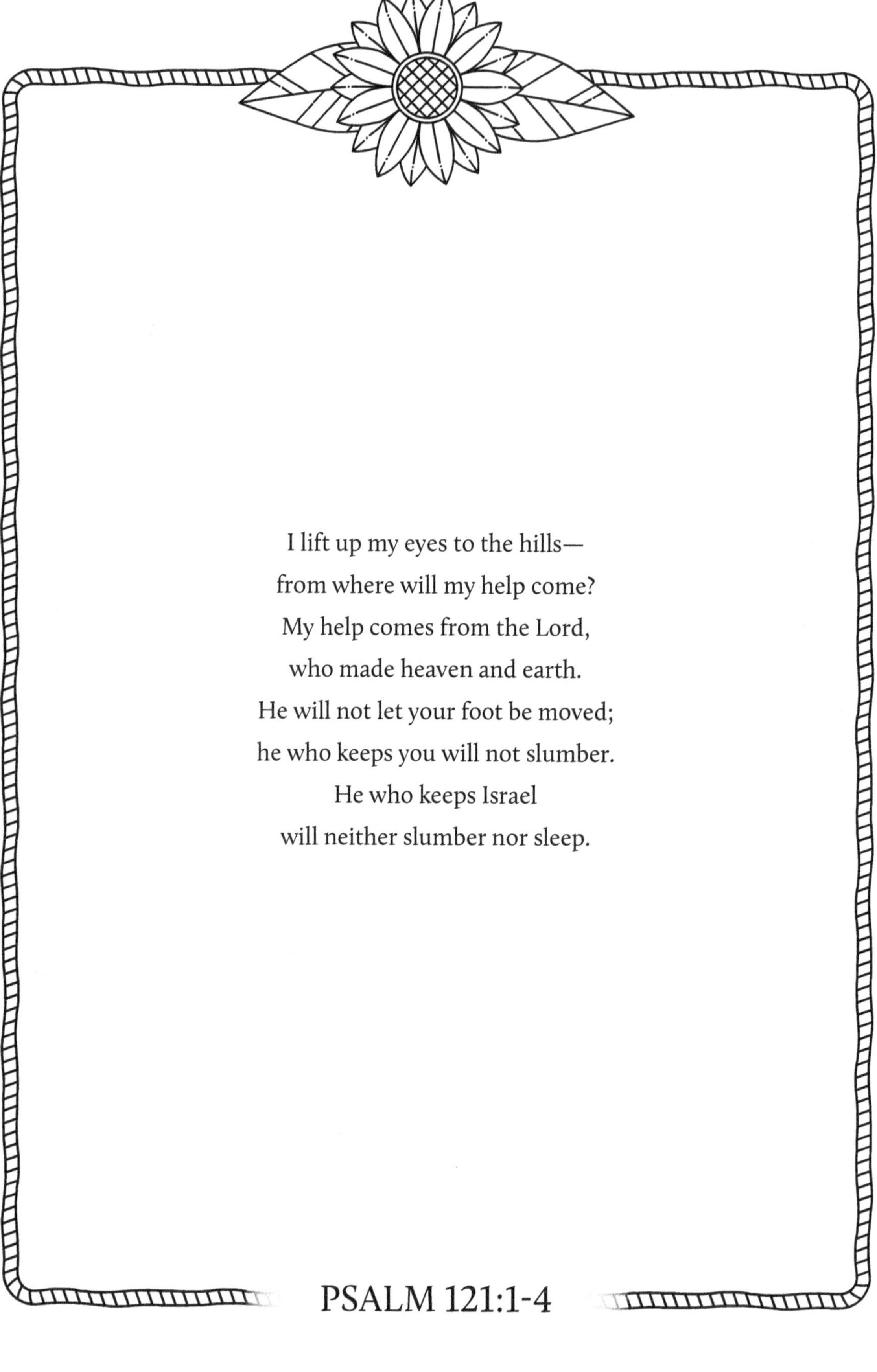

I lift up my eyes to the hills—
from where will my help come?
My help comes from the Lord,
who made heaven and earth.
He will not let your foot be moved;
he who keeps you will not slumber.
He who keeps Israel
will neither slumber nor sleep.

PSALM 121:1-4

My help comes from the Lord, who made heaven and earth.
Psalm 121:2

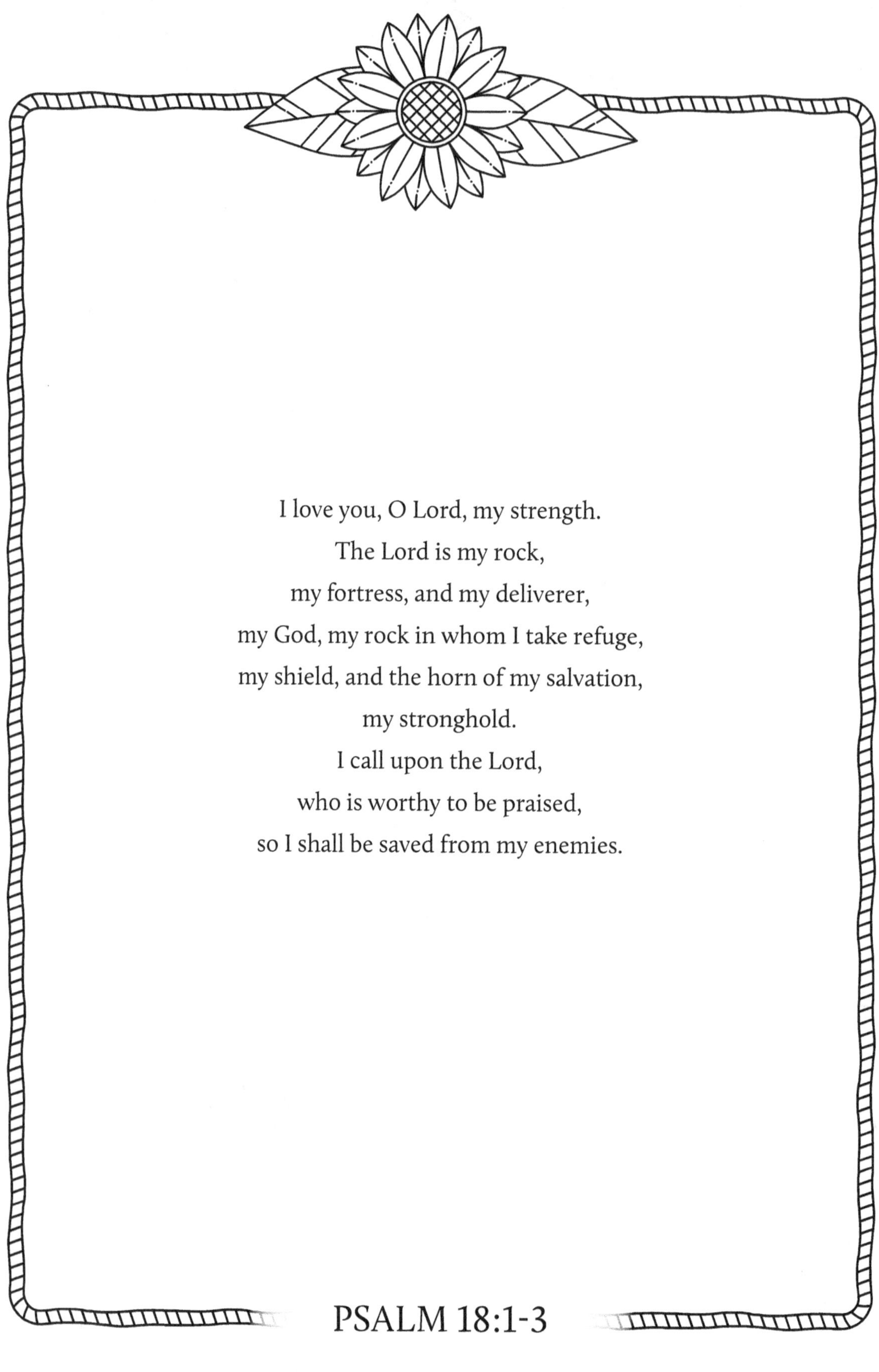

I love you, O Lord, my strength.

The Lord is my rock,

my fortress, and my deliverer,

my God, my rock in whom I take refuge,

my shield, and the horn of my salvation,

my stronghold.

I call upon the Lord,

who is worthy to be praised,

so I shall be saved from my enemies.

PSALM 18:1-3

I love you,
O Lord, my
strength
Psalm 18:1

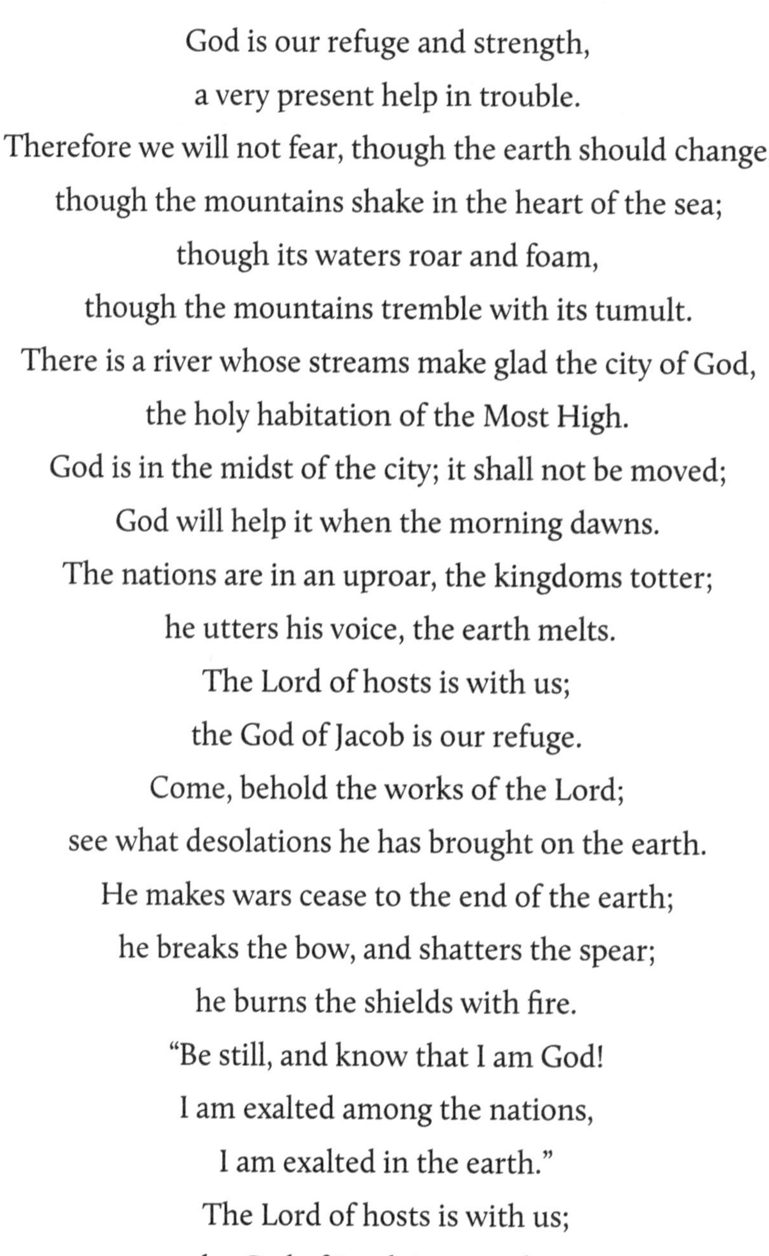

God is our refuge and strength,

a very present help in trouble.

Therefore we will not fear, though the earth should change,

though the mountains shake in the heart of the sea;

though its waters roar and foam,

though the mountains tremble with its tumult.

There is a river whose streams make glad the city of God,

the holy habitation of the Most High.

God is in the midst of the city; it shall not be moved;

God will help it when the morning dawns.

The nations are in an uproar, the kingdoms totter;

he utters his voice, the earth melts.

The Lord of hosts is with us;

the God of Jacob is our refuge.

Come, behold the works of the Lord;

see what desolations he has brought on the earth.

He makes wars cease to the end of the earth;

he breaks the bow, and shatters the spear;

he burns the shields with fire.

"Be still, and know that I am God!

I am exalted among the nations,

I am exalted in the earth."

The Lord of hosts is with us;

the God of Jacob is our refuge.

PSALM 46

Be still,
and know that
I am God!
Psalm 46:10

Keep me safe, my God, for in you I take refuge.

I say to the Lord, "You are my Lord;

apart from you I have no good thing."

I say of the holy people who are in the land,

"They are the noble ones in whom is all my delight."

Those who run after other gods will suffer more and more.

I will not pour out libations of blood to such gods

or take up their names on my lips.

Lord, you alone are my portion and my cup;

you make my lot secure.

The boundary lines have fallen for me in pleasant places;

surely I have a delightful inheritance.

I will praise the Lord, who counsels me;

even at night my heart instructs me.

I keep my eyes always on the Lord.

With him at my right hand, I will not be shaken.

Therefore my heart is glad and my tongue rejoices;

my body also will rest secure,

because you will not abandon me to the realm of the dead,

nor will you let your faithful one see decay.

You make known to me the path of life;

you will fill me with joy in your presence,

with eternal pleasures at your right hand.

PSALM 16:1-8

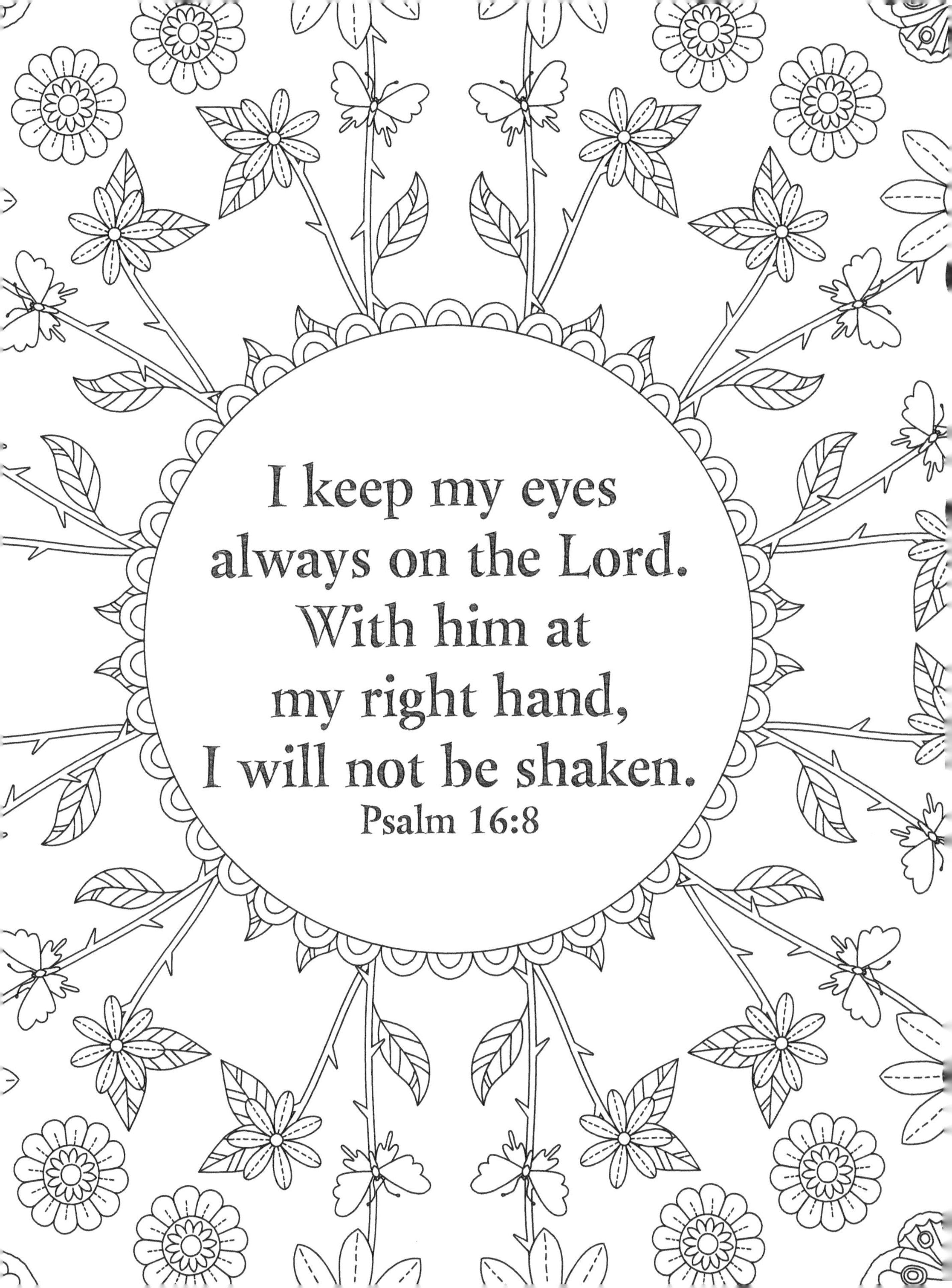

I keep my eyes
always on the Lord.
With him at
my right hand,
I will not be shaken.
Psalm 16:8

I give you thanks, O Lord, with my whole heart;

before the gods I sing your praise;

I bow down toward your holy temple

and give thanks to your name for your steadfast love

and your faithfulness;

for you have exalted your name and your word

above everything.

On the day I called, you answered me,

you increased my strength of soul.

All the kings of the earth shall praise you, O Lord,

for they have heard the words of your mouth.

They shall sing of the ways of the Lord,

for great is the glory of the Lord.

For though the Lord is high, he regards the lowly;

but the haughty he perceives from far away.

Though I walk in the midst of trouble,

you preserve me against the wrath of my enemies;

you stretch out your hand,

and your right hand delivers me.

The Lord will fulfill his purpose for me;

your steadfast love, O Lord, endures forever.

Do not forsake the work of your hands.

PSALM 138

The
Lord
will fulfill
His purpose
for me
Psalm 138:8

Fret not yourself because of the wicked,

be not envious of wrongdoers!

For they will soon fade like the grass,

and wither like the green herb.

Trust in the Lord, and do good;

so you will dwell in the land, and enjoy security.

Take delight in the Lord,

and he will give you the desires of your heart.

Commit your way to the Lord;

trust in him, and he will act.

He will bring forth your vindication as the light,

and your right as the noonday.

Be still before the Lord, and wait patiently for him;

fret not yourself over him who prospers in his way,

over the man who carries out evil devices!

PSALM 37:1-7

Commit
your ways
to the Lord;
trust in him,
and he will act.
Psalm 37:5

The Lord answer you in the day of trouble!
The name of the God of Jacob protect you!
May he send you help from the sanctuary,
and give you support from Zion.
May he remember all your offerings,
and regard with favor your burnt sacrifices.
May he grant you your heart's desire,
and fulfill all your plans.
May we shout for joy over your victory,
and in the name of our God set up our banners.
May the Lord fulfill all your petitions.

PSALM 20:1-5

MAY HE GRANT YOU
your heart's desire,
AND FULFIL
all your plans!
PSALM 20:4

How long, O Lord? Will you forget me forever?
How long will you hide your face from me?
How long must I bear pain in my soul,
and have sorrow in my heart all day long?
How long shall my enemy be exalted over me?
Consider and answer me, O Lord my God!
Give light to my eyes, or I will sleep the sleep of death,
and my enemy will say, "I have prevailed";
my foes will rejoice because I am shaken.

But I trusted in your steadfast love;
my heart shall rejoice in your salvation.
I will sing to the Lord,
because he has dealt bountifully with me.

PSALM 13

I WILL
sing
TO THE LORD,
BECAUSE HE HAS
BEEN good
TO ME.
PSALM 13:6

The Lord makes firm the steps
of the one who delights in him;
though he may stumble, he will not fall,
for the Lord upholds him with his hand.
I was young and now I am old,
yet I have never seen the righteous forsaken
or their children begging bread.
They are always generous and lend freely;
their children will be a blessing.
Turn from evil and do good;
then you will dwell in the land forever.
For the Lord loves the just
and will not forsake his faithful ones.

PSALM 37:23-28

The
Lord
makes
firm the steps
of the one who
delights
in Him
Psalm 37:23

The Lord is gracious and merciful,

slow to anger and abounding in steadfast love.

The Lord is good to all,

and his compassion is over all that he has made.

All your works shall give thanks to you, O Lord,

and all your faithful shall bless you.

They shall speak of the glory of your kingdom,

and tell of your power,

to make known to all people your mighty deeds,

and the glorious splendor of your kingdom.

Your kingdom is an everlasting kingdom,

and your dominion endures

throughout all generations.

The Lord is faithful in all his words,

and gracious in all his deeds.

The Lord upholds all who are falling,

and raises up all who are bowed down.

The eyes of all look to you,

and you give them their food in due season.

You open your hand,

satisfying the desire of every living thing.

PSALM 145:8-16

THE LORD IS
gracious &
merciful
PSALM 145:8

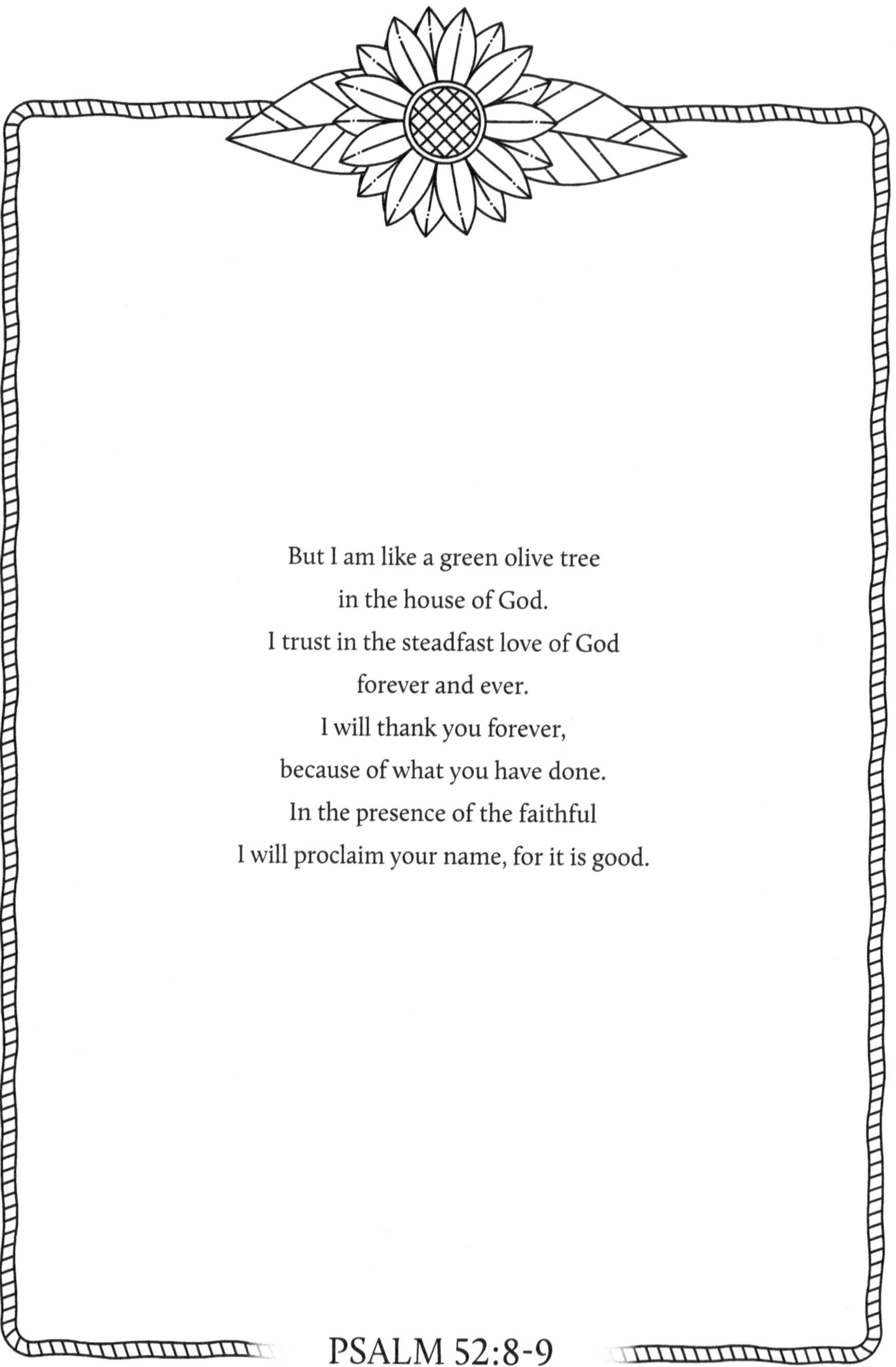

But I am like a green olive tree
in the house of God.
I trust in the steadfast love of God
forever and ever.
I will thank you forever,
because of what you have done.
In the presence of the faithful
I will proclaim your name, for it is good.

PSALM 52:8-9

I trust
IN THE
STEADFAST
LOVE OF GOD
forever
AND EVER.
PSALM 52:8

I love you, O Lord, my strength.

The Lord is my rock, my fortress, and my deliverer,

my God, my rock in whom I take refuge,

my shield, and the horn of my salvation, my stronghold.

I call upon the Lord, who is worthy to be praised,

so I shall be saved from my enemies.

The cords of death encompassed me;

the torrents of perdition assailed me;

the cords of Sheol entangled me;

the snares of death confronted me.

In my distress I called upon the Lord;

to my God I cried for help.

From his temple he heard my voice,

and my cry to him reached his ears.

PSALM 18:1-6

The Lord is
my rock,
my fortress,
& my deliverer,
my God, my rock
in whom I take refuge,
my shield,
and the horn of
my salvation,
my stronghold.

Psalm 18:2

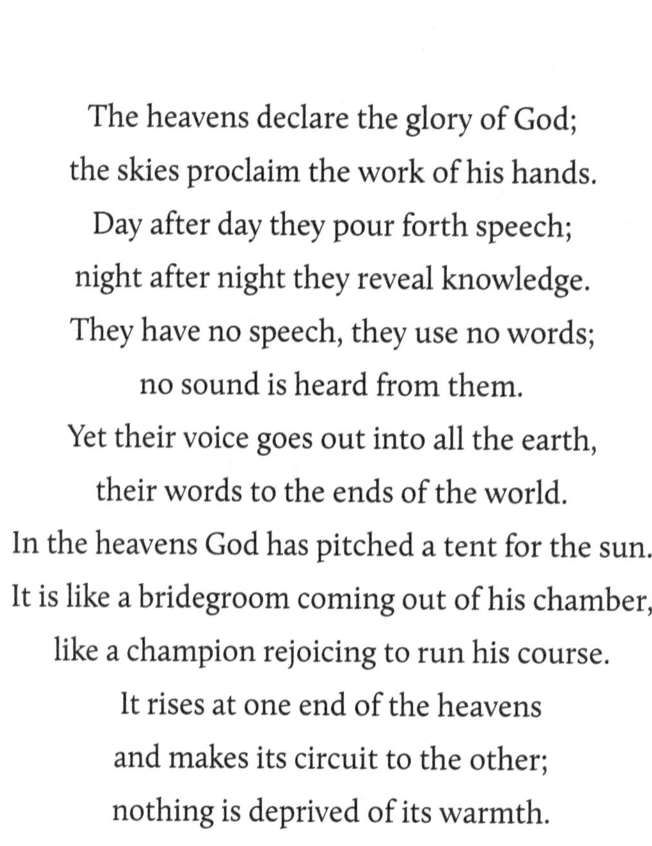

The heavens declare the glory of God;

the skies proclaim the work of his hands.

Day after day they pour forth speech;

night after night they reveal knowledge.

They have no speech, they use no words;

no sound is heard from them.

Yet their voice goes out into all the earth,

their words to the ends of the world.

In the heavens God has pitched a tent for the sun.

It is like a bridegroom coming out of his chamber,

like a champion rejoicing to run his course.

It rises at one end of the heavens

and makes its circuit to the other;

nothing is deprived of its warmth.

PSALM 19:1-6

The
heavens
declare the
Glory of God
Psalm 19:1

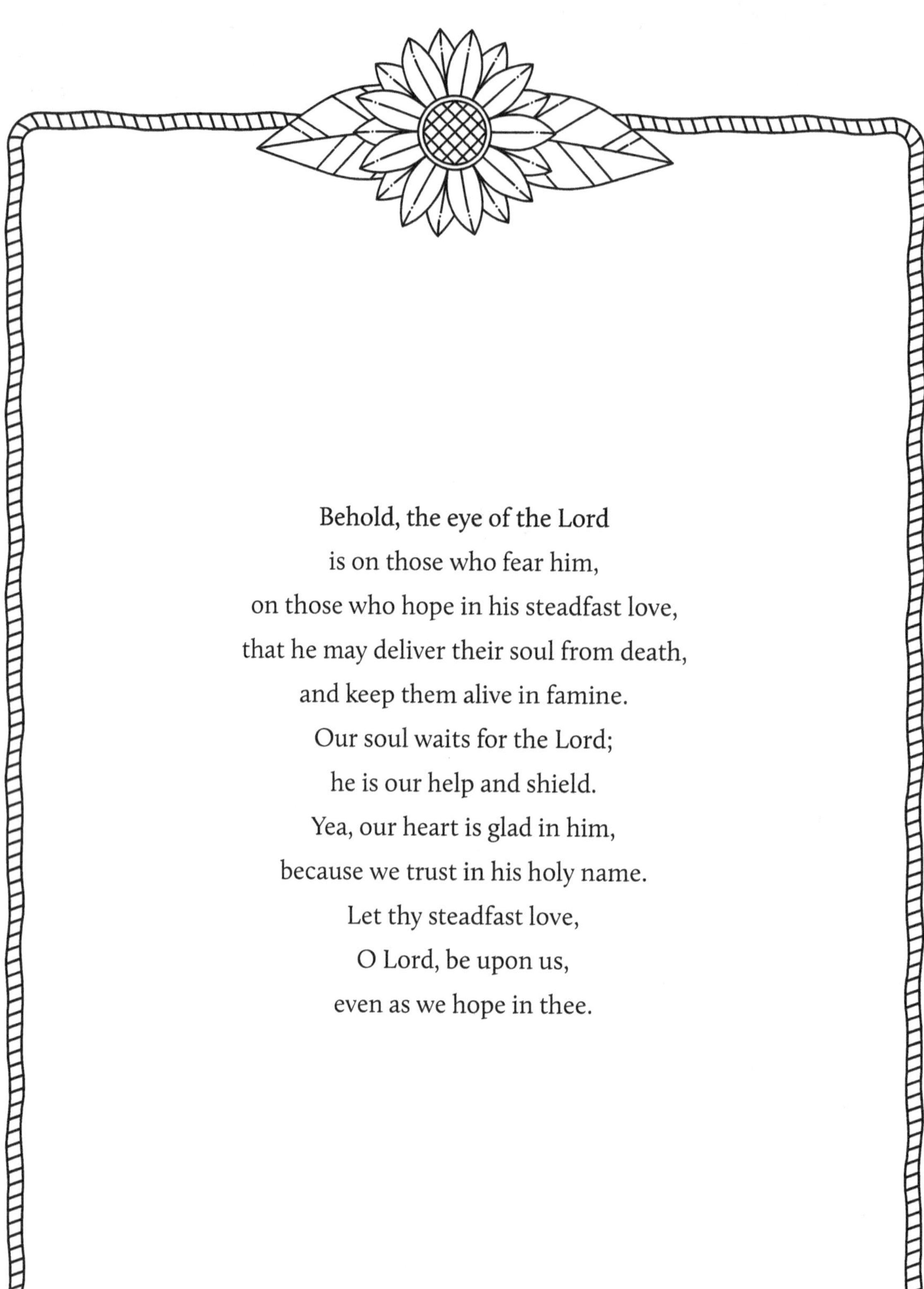

Behold, the eye of the Lord

is on those who fear him,

on those who hope in his steadfast love,

that he may deliver their soul from death,

and keep them alive in famine.

Our soul waits for the Lord;

he is our help and shield.

Yea, our heart is glad in him,

because we trust in his holy name.

Let thy steadfast love,

O Lord, be upon us,

even as we hope in thee.

PSALM 33:18-22

Our heart is glad in Him, because we trust in his holy name.
Psalm 33:21

O come, let us worship and bow down,

let us kneel before the Lord, our Maker!

For he is our God,

and we are the people of his pasture,

and the sheep of his hand.

O that today you would hearken to his voice!

Harden not your hearts, as at Meribah,

as on the day at Massah in the wilderness,

when your fathers tested me,

and put me to the proof,

though they had seen my work.

PSALM 95:6-9

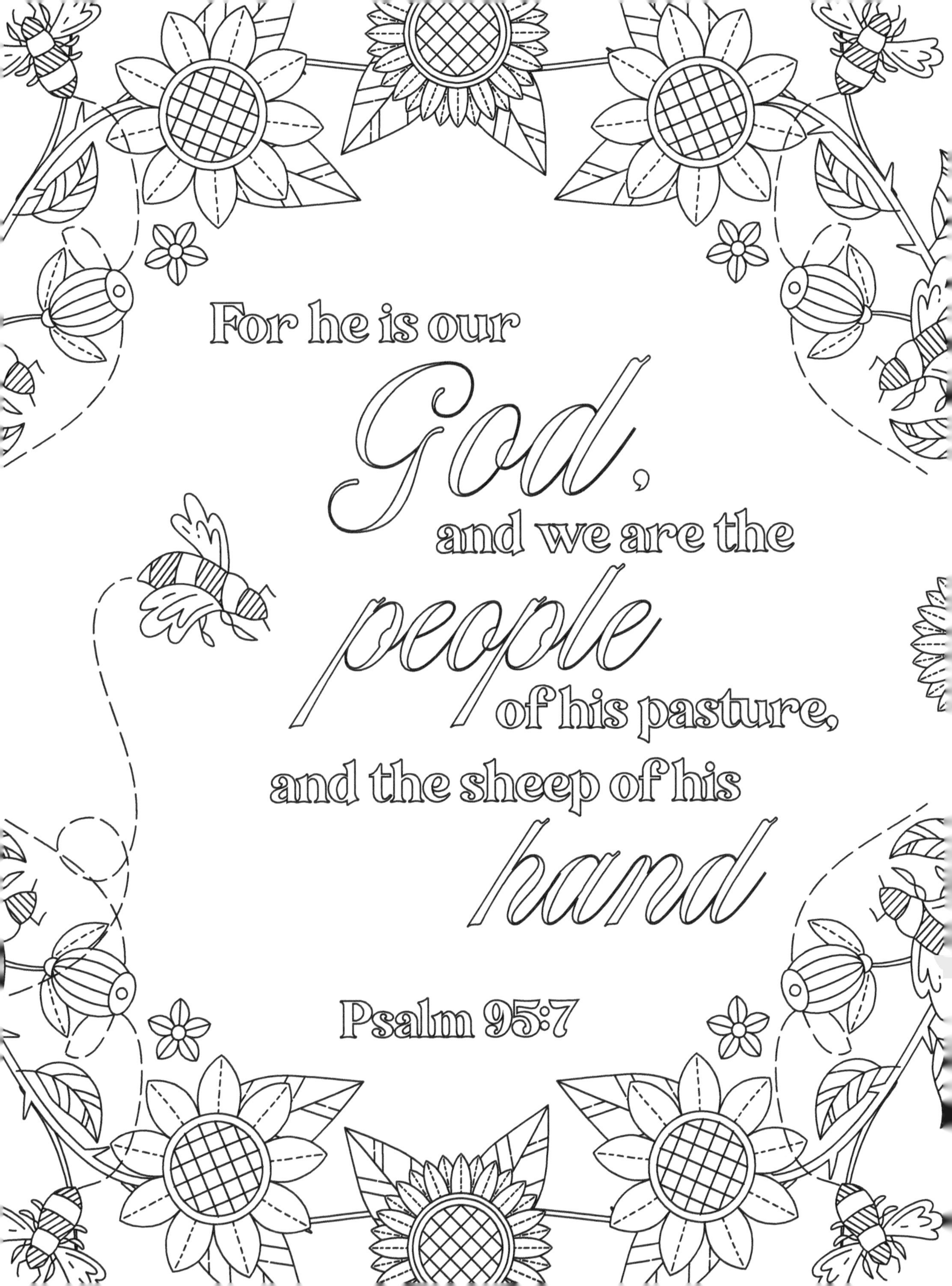

For he is our
God,
and we are the
people
of his pasture,
and the sheep of his
hand
Psalm 95:7

I will tell of the decree of the Lord:

He said to me, "You are my son;

today I have begotten you.

Ask of me, and I will make the nations your heritage,

and the ends of the earth your possession.

You shall break them with a rod of iron,

and dash them in pieces like a potter's vessel."

Now therefore, O kings, be wise;

be warned, O rulers of the earth.

Serve the Lord with fear,

with trembling kiss his feet,

or he will be angry, and you will perish in the way;

for his wrath is quickly kindled.

Happy are all who take refuge in him.

PSALM 2:7-12

Happy are all
who take refuge
in the Lord.

Psalm 2:12

The Lord is your keeper;

the Lord is your shade at your right hand.

The sun shall not strike you by day,

nor the moon by night.

The Lord will keep you from all evil;

he will keep your life.

The Lord will keep

your going out and your coming in

from this time on and forevermore.

PSALM 121:4-8

THE Lord WILL keep you FROM ALL HARM. PSALM 121:7

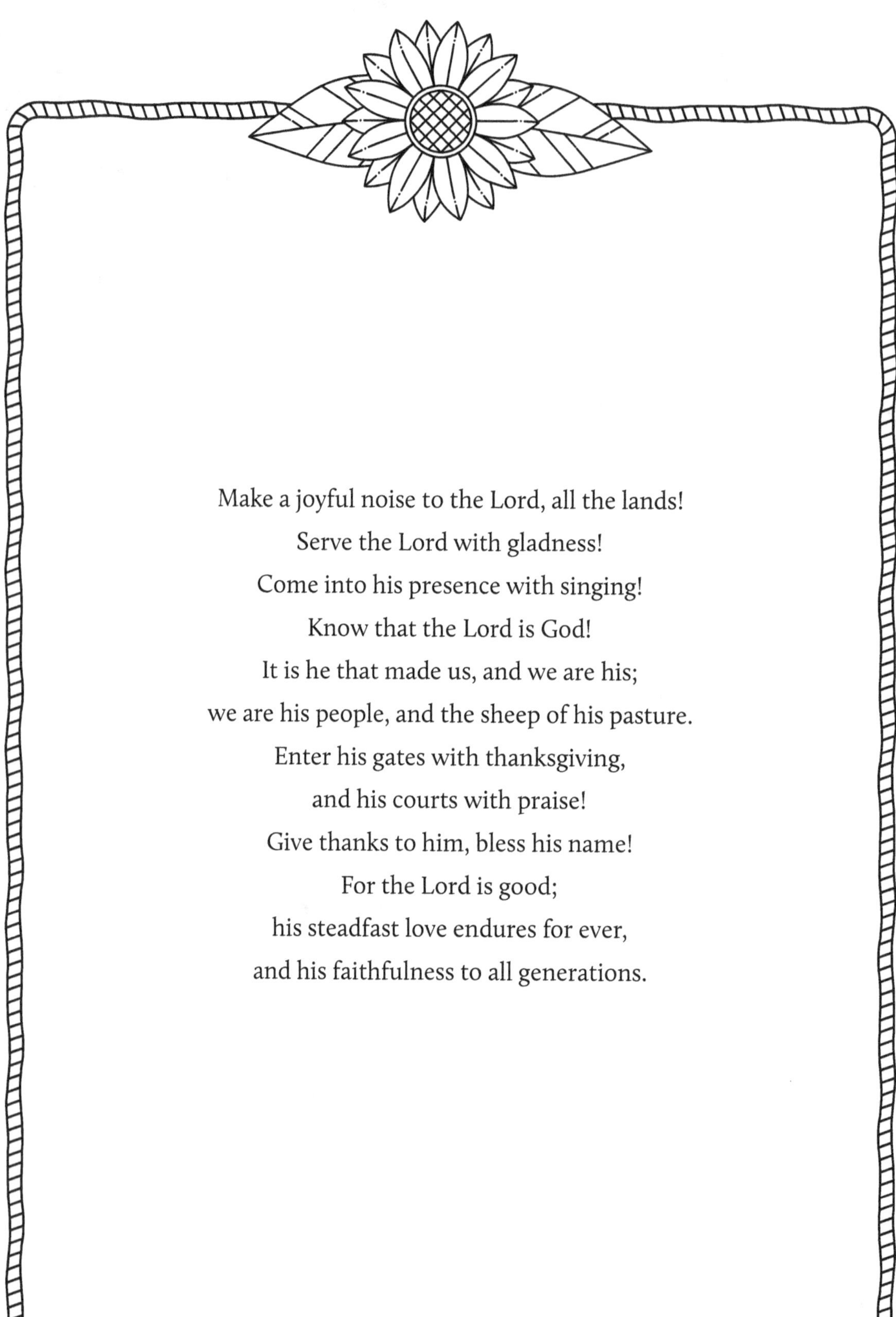

Make a joyful noise to the Lord, all the lands!

Serve the Lord with gladness!

Come into his presence with singing!

Know that the Lord is God!

It is he that made us, and we are his;

we are his people, and the sheep of his pasture.

Enter his gates with thanksgiving,

and his courts with praise!

Give thanks to him, bless his name!

For the Lord is good;

his steadfast love endures for ever,

and his faithfulness to all generations.

PSALM 100

For the Lord is good; his steadfast love endures forever, and his faithfulness to all generations.

Psalm 100:5

This is the day which the Lord has made;

let us rejoice and be glad in it.

Save us, we beseech thee, O Lord!

O Lord, we beseech thee, give us success!

Blessed be he who enters in the name of the Lord!

We bless you from the house of the Lord.

The Lord is God,

and he has given us light.

Bind the festal procession with branches,

up to the horns of the altar!

Thou art my God,

and I will give thanks to thee;

thou art my God, I will extol thee.

O give thanks to the Lord, for he is good;

for his steadfast love endures for ever!

PSALM 118:24-29

THIS IS
THE DAY
WHICH the
Lord
HAS MADE; LET US
rejoice
& be glad
IN IT
Psalm 118:24

Praise be to the Lord,

for he showed me the wonders of his love

when I was in a city under siege.

In my alarm I said,

"I am cut off from your sight!"

Yet you heard my cry for mercy

when I called to you for help.

Love the Lord, all his faithful people!

The Lord preserves those who are true to him,

but the proud he pays back in full.

Be strong and take heart,

all you who hope in the Lord.

PSALM 31:21-24

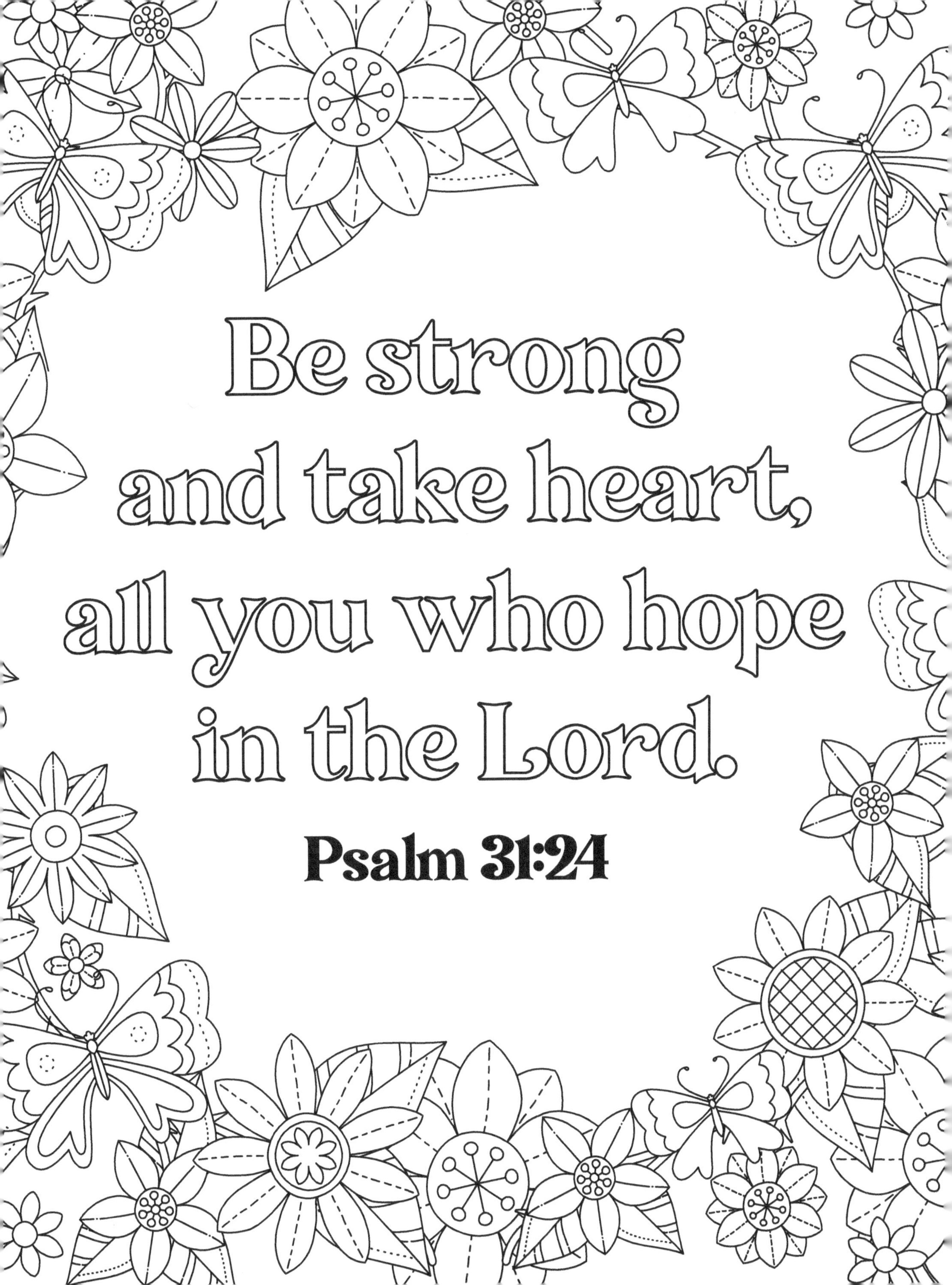

Be strong
and take heart,
all you who hope
in the Lord.
Psalm 31:24

The voice of the Lord makes the oaks to whirl,

and strips the forests bare;

and in his temple all cry, "Glory!"

The Lord sits enthroned over the flood;

the Lord sits enthroned as king for ever.

May the Lord give strength to his people!

May the Lord bless his people with peace!

PSALM 29:9-11

May the Lord
bless
his people with
peace!
Psalm 29:11

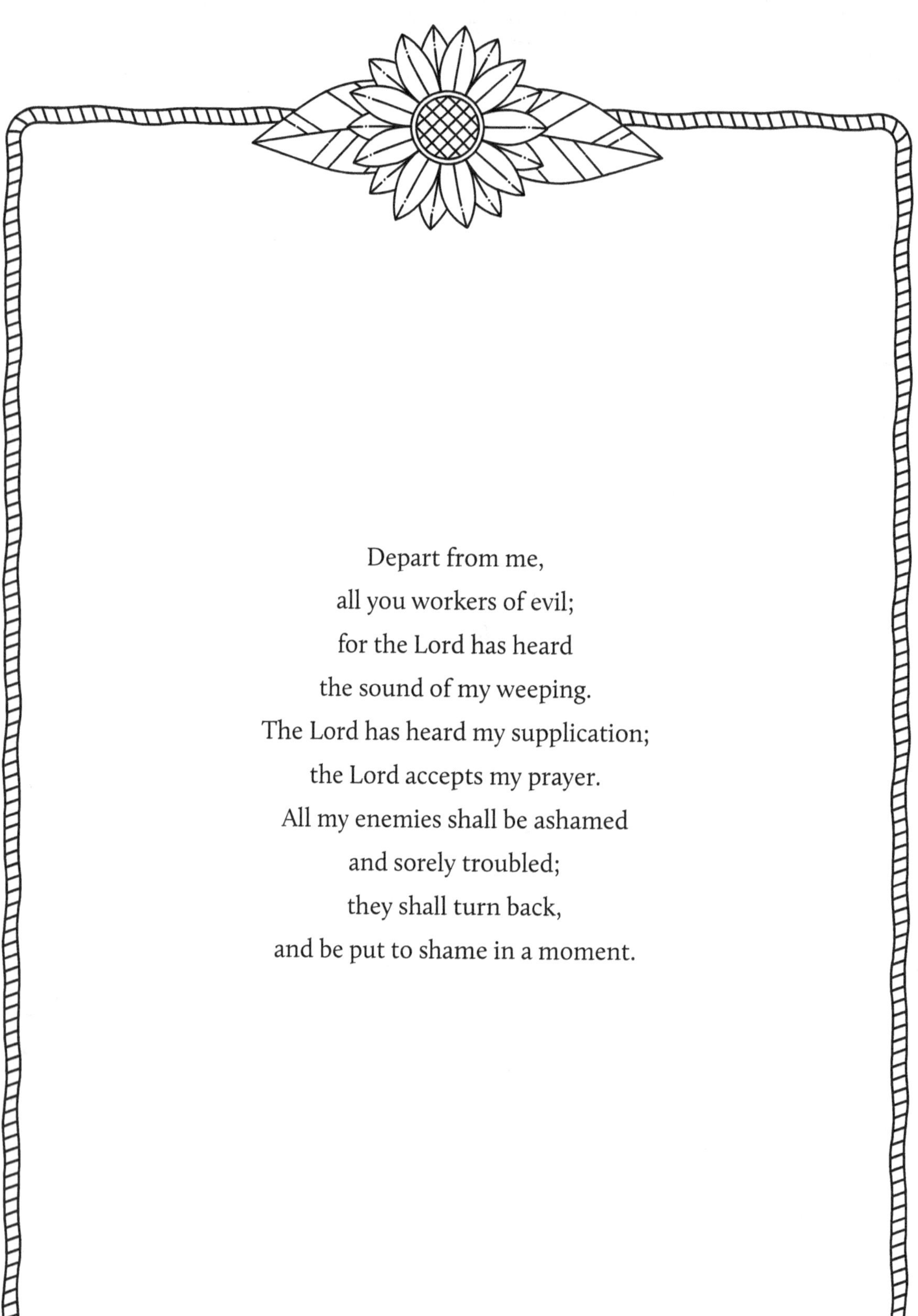

Depart from me,

all you workers of evil;

for the Lord has heard

the sound of my weeping.

The Lord has heard my supplication;

the Lord accepts my prayer.

All my enemies shall be ashamed

and sorely troubled;

they shall turn back,

and be put to shame in a moment.

PSALM 6:8-10

The Lord has heard my supplication; the Lord accepts my prayer.

Psalm 6:9

Make me to know thy ways, O Lord;

teach me thy paths.

Lead me in thy truth, and teach me,

for thou art the God of my salvation;

for thee I wait all the day long.

Be mindful of thy mercy,

O Lord, and of thy steadfast love,

for they have been from of old.

Remember not the sins of my youth,

or my trangressions;

according to thy steadfast love remember me,

for thy goodness' sake, O Lord!

PSALM 25:4-10

Make me to
know thy ways,
O Lord; teach me
thy paths.
Psalm 25:4

I waited patiently for the Lord;

he turned to me and heard my cry.

He lifted me out of the slimy pit,

out of the mud and mire;

he set my feet on a rock

and gave me a firm place to stand.

He put a new song in my mouth,

a hymn of praise to our God.

Many will see and fear the Lord

and put their trust in him.

Blessed is the one

who trusts in the Lord,

who does not look to the proud,

to those who turn aside to false gods.

Many, Lord my God,

are the wonders you have done,

the things you planned for us.

None can compare with you;

were I to speak and tell of your deeds,

they would be too many to declare.

PSALM 40:1-5

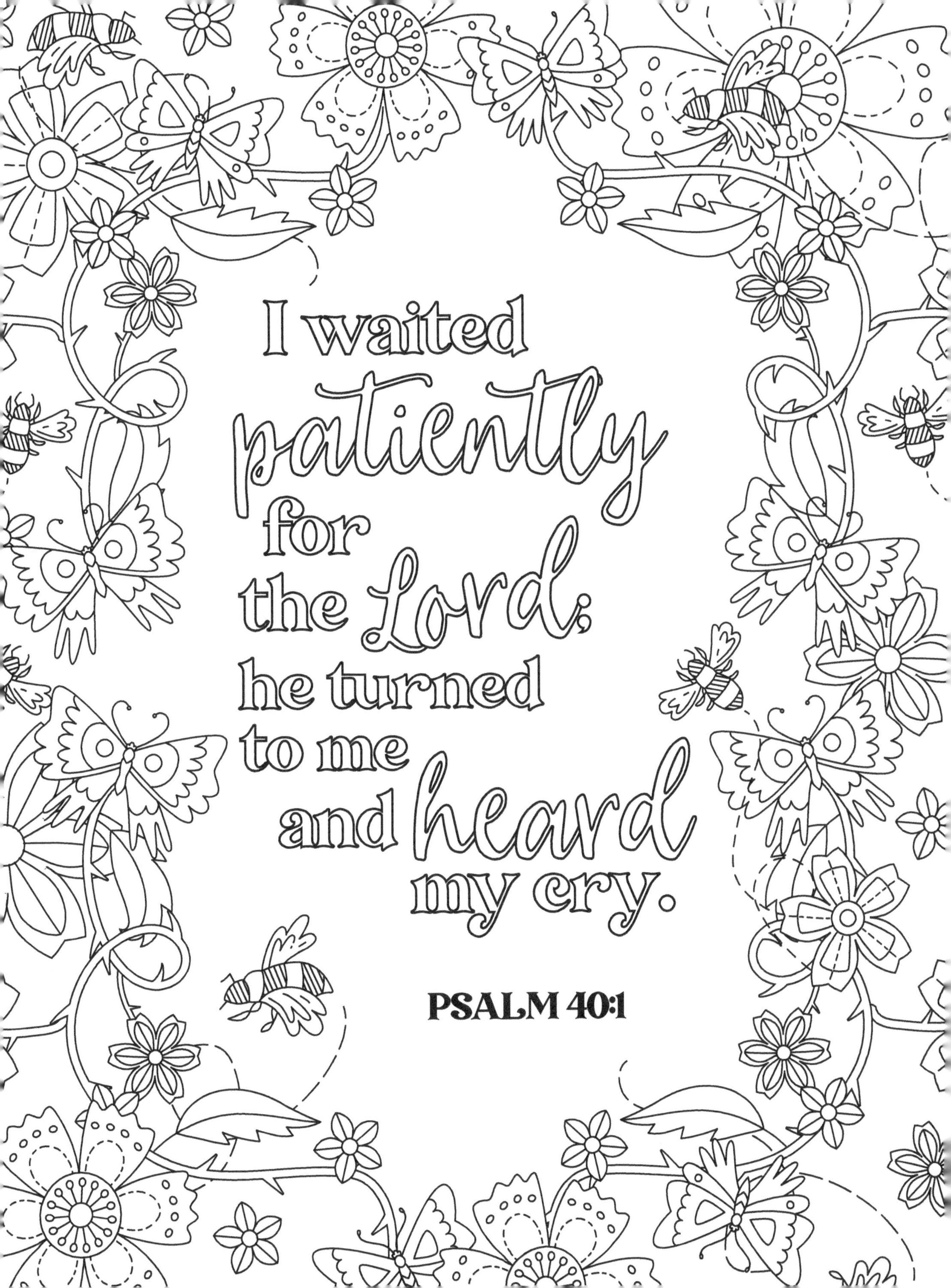

I waited patiently for the Lord; he turned to me and heard my cry.
PSALM 40:1

Therefore my heart is glad,

and my soul rejoices;

my body also dwells secure.

For thou dost not give me up to Sheol,

or let thy godly one see the Pit.

Thou dost show me the path of life;

in thy presence there is fullness of joy,

in thy right hand are pleasures for evermore.

PSALM 16:9-11

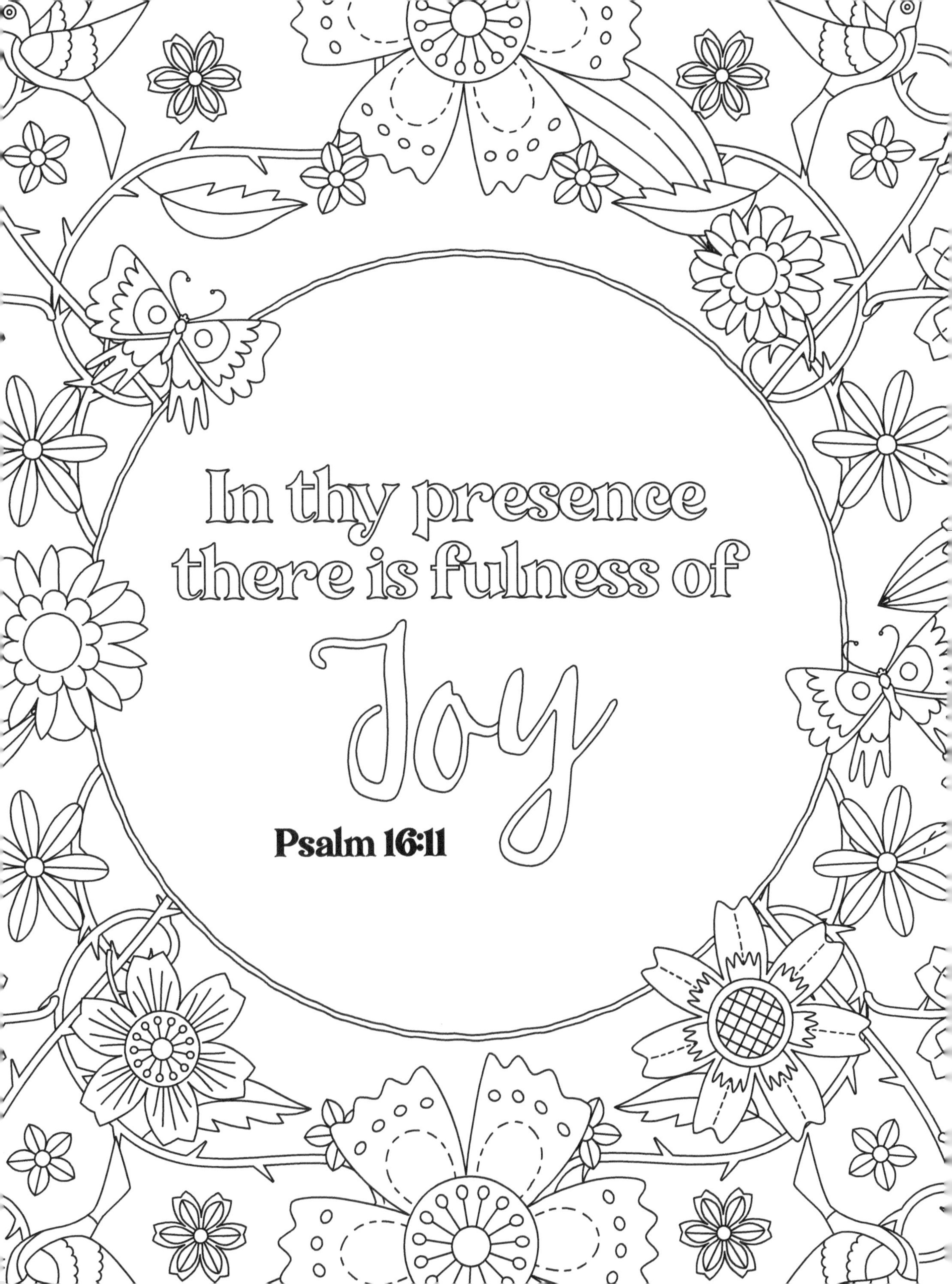

In thy presence
there is fulness of
Joy
Psalm 16:11